ESSEX COUNTY LIBRARY

Please see page iv for further copyright information

CRACKS

First performed at the Eugene O'Neill Theatre Center, Waterford, Connecticut on 31st July 1975, with the following cast:

Rick	Ben Masters
Sammy	Joe Grifasi
Nadine	Rosemary De Angelis
Jade	Meryl Streep
Clay	Ed Zang
Gideon	Christopher Lloyd
Maggie	Jill Andre
Roberta	Louis Giambalvo
Irene	Jill Eikenberry

Directed by Tony Giordano
Designed by Peter Larkin

The London première was at the King's Head Theatre on 29th April 1993, with the following cast:

Rick	Francois Testory
Sammy	Michael Higgs
Nadine	Jane Gurnett
Jade	Tracy Keating
Clay	Bradley Lavelle
Gideon	Ben Daniels
Maggie	Deborah Norton
Roberta	Peter Whitman
Irene	Briony Glassco

Directed by Tim Luscombe
Lighting by Nick Richings

CHARACTERS

Rick
Sammy
Nadine
Jade
Clay
Gideon
Maggie
Roberta
Irene

The action of the play takes place in the living-room, study and garden of Rick's house in California

Time – 1973

CRACKS

In the autumn of 1973 I was in Taos, New Mexico, where The Harriet Wurlitzer Foundation, an organization devoted to providing a retreat for young artists, had installed me in a house so I could experience the 'soothing calm' of my surroundings and hopefully write a play. Outside my house lay an astonishing physical and emotional landscape that featured breathtaking canyons and gorges and the Rio Grande — God's country, surely — and ancient Indian pueblos and Indian magic and Indian ceremonies and a sacred mountain forbidden to the white man and a fiercely alcoholic and unhappy Mexican community and an occasional sound of gunfire and wandering tribes of shell-shocked hippies mourning the sixties and a secret Catholic cult named Penitentes who each Easter crucified one of their members. New Mexico, in fact, has a singular law outlawing crucifixion. In this soothing calm, I wrote *Cracks*.

Taos was calm compared to The Eugene O'Neill Playwrights Foundation in Waterford, Connecticut where, in the summer of 1975, *Cracks* was first performed. The O'Neill is a unique testing ground for new plays and a rare and positive nurturing experience for young playwrights. For four bizarre weeks the entire American theatre swoops down on to 'Camp Eugene' and creates drama as intricate and heady off stage as on. *Cracks* was performed by a thrilling cast. The audience laughed and laughed. It caused a sensation. Although the O'Neill is supposed to be immune to commercial considerations, people kept dropping out of trees screaming 'smash hit, smash hit' at me. For someone whose work had been totally ignored until then, all this tree dropping seemed a bit surreal. But I did suddenly have many new friends. And dinner invitations. Back in New York strangers smiled at me on the street. Did I really hear them murmuring 'smash hit, smash hit'? I could even get a table at Joe Allen's.

Cracks opened off-Broadway at the Theatre DeLys the following winter. The producer was a fiery Spanish beauty with Titian hair, fractured English and an impressive bank account that at that stage of her life permitted her to produce plays and at a later stage landed her in prison for fraud. A not unnatural progression.

The first preview went reasonably well. There was work to do, but we had a week. Everyone seemed pleased — except our producer. 'Ze audience, zey laughed, zat is no good', she complained. 'But it's a comedy', the director replied. 'No, no, eet is serious drama. Eet has message', said the producer. 'I have good idea. We hire two actors. Zey dress like newsboys and run down aisles during interval carrying newspapers and shout "Extra, Extra — read all about eet," and zen zey read out ze message of ze play.' She never did reveal what she assumed the message was, but she did solemnly promise us that 'by opening night, zher will be no laughter'. That was possibly the first promise our producer ever kept.

The week that followed was harrowing. The highpoint occurred when the producer presented a twelve-year-old student who was 'interested in theatre' and had ideas for rewrites. Neither his ideas nor the newsboys were accepted, but then there was no need — my own rewrites, conceived in confusion and mounting chaos, were horrific enough. The director, loyal and loving to the play, had to spend most of his energy coping with the tantrums of the producer, and the cast, morale diving, became steadily unsteady. At each performance, the audience laughed less.

Opening night, I lay in a back aisle, coiled in a foetal ball, listening to the stunning, spectacular sound of silence. You could hear a pin drop. You shouldn't hear pins drop in comedies. The reviews the next day would have embarrassed Klaus Barbie. Never let a New York critic smell blood. The smash hit was a disaster. My new friends rushed back into the genie's bottle, clutching the dinner invitations. People actually crossed over the road rather than speak to me. I wasn't even allowed into Joe Allen's bar. Such is failure in New York. The experience proved profitable when years later I had a 'success' in the same city. By then I knew that it mattered not if they were throwing confetti or tomatoes — the best thing to do was to duck and get on with it.

Martin Sherman

ACT I
SCENE 1

Rick is alone on stage. He is twenty-nine, has a wild face and a beautiful, sinewy body. He is almost naked. He takes a stick of white make-up and paints the area around his right eye white. He draws a jagged orange line down his chest. He colours his loins green. He wraps a purple sash around his body. He puts a silver bracelet on one arm, a golden bracelet on the other. He drapes a necklace of turquoise and coral on his chest. He takes a knife and slits his arm, beneath the golden bracelet, and covers his neck with blood. He smiles. He holds his hands out — in supplication — then brings them together and claps twice. His right leg moves out to one side. His left leg to the other side. A dance has begun. His face is bathed in ecstasy. A shot rings out. Rick falls to the ground, dead

Black-out

SCENE 2

The Lights rise on Rick's house. An early summer evening. California, 1973

The living-room is to the R. It is well-spaced, comfortable, surprisingly uncluttered, with a bar, closet and fireplace, table, coffee table and telephone. A few rather bizarre paintings hang on the walls. A staircase, UC, leads to the second floor. A window is next to the stairway. The garden can be slightly glimpsed, off R. A doorway leads from the garden to the living-room. Rick's study adjoins the living-room, a door linking the two. Another door in the study, far L, leads to a bathroom. There are two bay windows in the study, which open to a veranda

As the Lights rise, party sounds are heard coming from the garden. The door from the living-room to the study is closed and all the windows in the house are open. Rick's body lies on the floor of the study

A man and a woman — Sammy and Nadine — waltz into the living-room from the garden. He is thirty-one, long—haired, very Jewish looking. She is twenty-eight, exceedingly vulnerable, with haunted eyes. There is no music. They hum a waltz to themselves in light accompaniment, dance around the room, and off again, into the garden

Jade enters. She is seventeen, dressed in feathers and jewellery

Clay follows her in. He is thirty-eight, distinguished-looking

Jade You know what I did the first time I met Rick? It was in my father's house. I was fifteen. My father was producing Rick's television special. I took Rick into my room and we smoked two joints, and he was just standing there in the doorway, and I did something I'd never done before, I took off all my clothes, and lay on the couch and played with my body and he said 'I don't believe you're doing this' and I kept rolling over and I got up and went to him and he had a whopping hard-on, so of course we had mad sex, and afterwards, he took me out and bought me a hot-fudge sundae and then I went home and read some spiritual books for a couple of hours, before I went to sleep. (*She looks around the room*) Where is he?

Clay He's busy. I'd like to get my camera. I'd like to put you on tape. All right? (*He smiles and takes her hand*)

They leave. Gideon enters. He is thirty, kind of freaky, very stoned. He sits on a sofa and lights a joint

The dancers return, waltz around the room again, still humming and waltz off

Maggie enters. She is forty-two, garishly dressed and somewhat dramatic. She carries a glass of egg-nog

Maggie Is Rick in his study?

Gideon He's working.

Maggie I want to see him.

Gideon (*taking her hand*) Ahh, let him be.

Maggie You were looking at me.

Gideon When?

Maggie Before.

Gideon Maybe.

Maggie I know you find me attractive. But just now, Rick's all I can handle. He goes down on me and everything. My last boyfriend didn't go down on me. He wasn't normal.

She wanders off into the garden. Roberta enters. Roberta is forty-five, and appears to be a man, a rather bulky man, but he is wearing a prim skirt and blouse, and his hair is in a neat little bun. He smokes a cigar

Roberta Rick? Hey, Rick, where the fuck are you? The party is getting rowdy. If you don't come out soon, I'm gonna bust a few heads.

He returns to the garden. Irene enters. She is twenty-nine, dressed more sedately than the others

Irene Where's Rick?

Gideon Rehearsing a new number.

Irene Gee, in the middle of a party?

Gideon That's his way. (*He holds out the joint*) Want some?

Irene No, thanks.

Gideon You don't like it here?

Irene (*smiling*) Oh, it's what I expected.

The couple dance in again. Once more around the room, and they stop, laughing. Sammy bows to Nadine

Nadine Thank you. I had a wonderful time. (*Her voice assumes another tone*) I was bored. (*Her natural tone*) Oh, shut up.

Embarrassed, she returns to the garden.

Sammy (*watching her leave*) Very weird. (*To Irene*) Want to dance?

Irene There's no music.

Sammy (*to Gideon*) How about you?

Gideon Nah.

Sammy You've got a pretty ass.

Gideon (*smiling*) Hey, man ... thanks.

Irene (*to Sammy*) Is it true that ... (*She stops herself*)

Sammy What?

Irene You know.

Sammy It's true.
Irene It doesn't make sense. I can't picture you entering a monastery.
Sammy Because I'm Jewish?
Irene Gosh. That's the least of it.

Roberta enters, agitated

Roberta Where is the shmuck? People are driving the wrong cars home. I'm gonna lay someone out.

Maggie enters

Maggie Cool it, Roberta. Party's almost over. I'll make you a drink.

Maggie goes to the bar

Jade and Clay enter. Clay is carrying a video camera and camera-lights. Jade goes to Irene

Jade You're Rick's cousin, right?
Irene Right.
Jade Want to come to my room?
Irene I don't think so.
Jade I'm really into families.

Nadine enters

Nadine Everyone's gone. Where's Rick? (*In her other tone*) Who cares? (*Her natural tone*) I care.

Suddenly there is a rumbling sound. The Lights flicker, go off, come on again. The entire house seems to be shaking. Then, just as suddenly, it stops

Maggie Oh my God! What was that?
Clay It's all right. Just a slight tremor. No harm.
Irene No harm? The whole room shook.
Gideon (*handing her the joint*) Here.
Nadine It happens a lot.

Irene You people are crazy, living in this place.

Jade (*walking to the study*) Rick, did you feel the earthquake? (*She opens the door and enters the study*) Rick?

Gideon Leave him alone.

Jade (*seeing the body*) Rick ...

Irene I mean, aren't you all afraid of dying? I could never live here. It doesn't make sense.

Jade (*kneeling over the body*) Rick...

Clay You get used to it.

Jade (*returning to the living-room*) Hey, it's very heavy in there. Rick's dead.

Black-out

SCENE 3

A few minutes later

Clay is filming Jade; the lights on his camera shine on her face

Clay Jade.

Jade Once. I wanted to be a dancer. My father sent me to ballet school. I practised every day. But then I had a spiritual revelation, and I stopped dancing, because, you see, it's easier to fuck. Fucking is easier than writing a poem, cooking a meal or weaving a rug, all of which I wanted to do at one time. Fucking is easier than falling in love. It means you're living in the now — no future, no past, no hangs, no worries. And Rick ... well, Rick *is* fucking. He's cock. He's an ice-cream cone with two flavours and jimmies on the top. Sometimes I remember that I'm seventeen and I wonder what it's like to be a little girl again and I think I've lived almost all of my life already, but then I get back into the 'now', and it's all right. I could kill Rick then, those dark times, but they never last.

Clay switches off the camera lights, bringing them up moments later on Maggie's face

Clay Maggie.

Maggie This is foolish. I wouldn't really kill him. I don't have a motive.

Clay You're an actress.

Jade Pretend.

Maggie When did you last see me *act*? Oh, I used to. For years. Off-Broadway, summer stock, road companies, learning my craft, becoming really good. Got me nowhere. One day I looked around and saw what was happening. *Crazy* was happening. So I made myself into a loon. Got invited everywhere. Now I'm no longer an actress. I'm a *star*. I go to openings, closings, funerals, parties, seminars, ballgames, races, marches, meetings, birthdays, weddings, street-fairs, rodeos — as long as there's a camera, or a reporter, to record it. A star! And Rick? Well, baby, the biggest star of us all. He's more than a good lay, you know what I mean? He's good publicity! As soon as I have an orgasm, I phone the papers. You know — I make it into a funny story. The whole fucockta world cares about us. But listen, I'm not dumb. He's tiring of the older woman bit. (*Slightly* older.) He's gonna move on. Well — not now! I'm gonna be The Lady in Black. I'll be up to my ass in flowers, and tears, and urns, and syndicated columns about our last sublime moments together. And if I'm lucky, I can milk it for at least six months. So? How's *that* for a motive?

Clay switches off the camera lights, bringing them up moments later on Sammy's face

Clay Sammy.

Sammy Sure, I could have killed him. You know when I met Rick? Ten years ago. In a small southern town, the night of a civil rights march. Oh yeah, I was big in civil rights. Honey, I registered *more* voters than the whole Department of Justice. Big favour I did them! Anyhow, Rick was just starting, singing kind of straight then. He had a concert scheduled in town that night. What did he know? Boy, even then he was sexy. Fucked me up. Fucked me up — and down, actually, but that's another story. No, it's not. It's what it's all about. He was mean, physically *mean*. And I dug it. That was the beginning of of my disorientation. Afterward, nothing seemed like exactly what it was. Well, civil rights became complicated, weren't no place for a white boy no more, and there were other things to drift into: flowers, honey. I wore flowers in my hair for years, and speed in my brain and always, at intervals, I'd come back to Rick, and he'd fuck me up and down again, and I'd leave, always more confused than before. You see, Rick made me turn to religion. If I had found Satan so *easily*, why not look for God? Oh, I looked in strange places. Like all good Jewish boys, I became a Buddhist. But that's obscure, very obscure. So I became a Catholic, which is easy, they'll take *anyone*. And one day, while I was floating through France, I came upon this cute town with a divine Benedictine mission. I badgered them for two years and finally they accepted me as a novice. It's their custom — if you're enough of a yenta they'll accept you. So Tuesday I fly Air France to become a monk. I'm even gonna give up outside fucking. Only do it with other monks. And you know, I'm really into it, into God and things. Now, I know that's a little convoluted, but I think that's reason enough to kill Rick.

Clay switches off the camera lights, bringing them up moments later on Nadine's face

Clay Nadine.

Nadine I was a student doing my thesis on 'The Psychology of Rock'. I went to interview Rick, and well, one thing led to another ... I guess I never got the interview. After a couple of weeks of travelling with Rick, a paper on the psychology of anything seemed absurd, so I left school, and also, I left group therapy, although Cynthia didn't want me to go — Cynthia was my analyst, a nice middle-aged lady ... Well, I got into a lot of different scenes — communes, ashrams — for a while all I did was milk goats — and then, some heavy relationships and some real bad drugs — lots of changes, I was very loose and not really *motivated*, you know. Then one day I bumped into his kid who had been in my group and he told me that Cynthia had killed herself. A lot of analysts commit suicide these days. It's sort of the logical conclusion of their work. Well, I was very struck by this ... I guess I felt guilty, maybe if I had stayed in group, I could have helped her. I began thinking about her all the time, and then one day ... (*Her voice assumes the other tone*) Don't tell them. (*Her natural tone*) Oh. That's Cynthia. One day she entered my body. Her spirit, that is. You know — a dybbuk. Well, we've been together ever since, and while it's been difficult, I think, in my way, I've been able to help.

Clay How about Rick?

Nadine Oh, I would never kill him. When I needed help, he gave me money, and he lets me crash in this house. He's really the only person who's been good to me. (*As Cynthia*) What do you think I've been? (*As herself*) Lay off it, will you, Cynthia? (*As Cynthia*) You've always misplaced your affections. (*As herself*) Lay off ... (*As Cynthia*) Why can't you see Rick for what he is? He likes to encourage your eccentricities, that's all. He doesn't really care about you. (*As herself*) Stop it! (*As Cynthia*) I hate the bastard! (*As herself*) I would never kill Rick. *Cynthia* would.

Clay switches off the camera lights, bringing them up moments later on Gideon's face

Clay Gideon.
Gideon The light's too bright. Turn it down. OK, man. I know what you're thinking. Jealousy. Poor Gideon playing his guitar two steps out of the spotlight, while Rick stands stage centre, getting all the attention with his jerk-off routines. Poor Gideon. Shit, man, poor Gideon had a good time. Good music, good dope, good chick ... I loved it, the whole ten-year gig. I didn't want it to end. I'd have to be crazy to kill him. Ah! Maybe *that's* it. Think whatever you want. I don't care.

Clay switches off the camera lights, bringing them up moments later on Roberta's face

Clay Roberta.
Roberta The guy was a creep. Still, he took me in when no-one wanted me. Yeah, I had a rough time. All those headlines — 'Docker Changes Sex!' Ahh, people are pigs, they don't understand. You see, it's not related to sex drives — you got that? It's just biological, I wasn't the gender my body said it was, see, and it got embarrassing, being on the docks, you know, and wearing dresses. But they got this operation now and they fix you up good. I'm much happier, I got to say that, *much* happier. Oh yeah — well, he needed a bodyguard, all those screaming kids at this concerts, trying to get on stage, touch him, pull his clothes apart. He was surrounded by a lot of weirdoes, I'll tell you that. I mean, his friends too. Perverts. Made me nervous. Sure, if I got good and mad, I could have totalled him. Why not?

Clay switches off the camera lights, bringing them up moments later on Irene's face

Clay Irene.

Irene I'd rather not.

Clay Go on. Everyone else has.

Irene Gosh, I had no reason to kill Rick. I hadn't seen him for years. He's asked me to come visit a lot, but my husband, Barry, doesn't approve of him, so this trip, with Barry away and everything, was my first chance... Barry's an army career man and Rick — well, he dances around with rattlesnakes and whips, and sings in falsetto. They're not used to that at Fort Myers. Why do you think he was painting his whole body like that? You know, when Rick was on stage, he didn't make any sense, not to me. I always want things to be logical, but just because he wasn't Andy Williams is no reason to kill him. I'm sorry. I don't have a motive.

Clay You grew up with him. There has to be something.

Irene Oh — well — we were kids together, you know how kids are. What do you want me to tell you, that he pulled my braids? Sure, he pulled my braids. And in the third grade he used to report me all the time to Miss Lane for talking; Miss Lane was deaf; she didn't know *who* was talking; I always had to stay after school. And if that's a motive, you're welcome to it.

Clay switches off the camera lights

Clay (*in darkness*) Someone take the camera.

Sammy takes the camera and lights and brings the light up on Clay's face

Sammy Clay.

Clay I used to be Rick's lawyer. Drug busts, paternity suits, indecent exposure ... the usual stuff. I was a very *good* lawyer. I won a famous case before the Supreme Court. The Bruno Decision. It meant that policemen had to show their badge number at the exact moment of arrest. My wife was especially proud of me; she believed in just causes. She was Navajo. I took her away from her reservation, away from the clear sky, into the city. One night, coming home from a concert, she was robbed and raped and stabbed. She died five days later. They caught the guy. A junkie. He went on trial, but he got off on a technicality. The policeman had neglected to show his badge number at the exact moment of arrest. The Bruno Decision. I lost interest in law. I was pretty low. That was the first time I took acid. While I was tripping, I heard a voice, very clearly, saying, 'Clay, you should get into pornography.' So I bought a movie camera and got some friends together ... Now I make the biggest grossing adult films in the country. What the hell. (*Pause*) Oh yes — Rick. Rick owns fifty per cent of my film company. Now I can have it all.

Sammy switches off the camera lights

Scene 4

The Lights rise on the house. Clay is putting the camera down and dismantling the lights, aided by Sammy. Nadine is in the study, sitting next to Rick's body. Gideon is smoking a joint and Maggie is pacing. Jade is sitting in a yoga position. Roberta is guarding the garden doors. Irene walks to the telephone

Irene I think we should try the police again.
Nadine (*staring at Rick*) He looks so sad.

Gideon takes the telephone, tries it

Gideon The lines are still dead.
Roberta Someone cut them, huh?
Gideon It was just a tremor. It often happens.
Sammy If there's a police station nearby, I can drive over ...
Irene What a good idea!
Roberta Nobody leaves the house! One of you jerks is a killer.
Irene That's ridiculous. There were at least twenty other people at the party.
Maggie Oh God! I forgot about them! I really thought it was one of us. Maybe even me. Is the egg-nog still in the garden? (*She goes to the garden door*)
Roberta I said nobody leaves.
Maggie Relax. I'm just going a few feet.

Roberta lets her pass. Maggie goes into the garden

Irene walks into the study

Sammy I think we should make a list of the people at the party, before we all forget.

Clay It does make sense that the killer would leave. That's a shame, I got such nice motives on film. Oh well.

He takes a bunch of writing pads from the coffee table and gives one each to Gideon, Jade and Roberta

Write down who you remember.
Irene (*looking at Rick's body*) I hardly knew him. I never had a brother. He was *like* a brother. That was a long time ago. We all grow up and lose each other. It's a shame.
Nadine Maybe we should cover him.
Irene I'll get a sheet.
Nadine No. A blanket. Something pretty.

Irene leaves the study and walks up the stairs to the second floor

Maggie returns to the living-room with a large bowl of egg-nog. She puts the bowl on a table and pours herself a cup

The others are absorbed, trying to remember names, occasionally writing on their pads

Gideon (*looking up*) Do you remember who that bearded cat was?
Jade Brown hair?
Gideon Yeah.
Jade Oleg. He's Russian. You know what he told me? He said he fucked his cat, and he's worried that the cat is pregnant. I think he shoots up though so it may not be true.
Maggie Put his name at the top of the list, with a star by it!

Sammy puts his pad down and walks into the study. Maggie picks up Sammy's pad and starts to write a name. Nadine is singing Swing Low, Sweet Chariot *softly to Rick. Sammy watches her*

Sammy Don't you think we should leave him alone?
Nadine No. I'm his friend. The others aren't. Except maybe you.
Sammy Yeah. Maybe. It's awful. I want to touch his body. I want to make love to him right now. Do you think that's the worst thought I'll ever have?
Nadine I think it's beautiful. I think you should.

Sammy Look, there's blood on his neck.

Nadine He was starting a song that way. He told me about it.

Sammy Oh. Right. His act. I forget about his act.

Nadine (*as Cynthia*) It was all an act. (*As herself*) Please leave us alone, Cynthia. Just this once. (*As Cynthia*) I don't like it here.

Sammy Maybe she's afraid.

Nadine Of what?

Sammy Another dead spirit.

Maggie looks up from her pad

Maggie There's that dwarf who used to be with the Peace Corps and now she's an embalmer...

Gideon Harriet Perlow.

Maggie Right. (*She writes it down*)

Nadine Can't you do something religious over him?

Sammy I haven't learned how yet.

Clay looks up from his pad

Clay How about that young man with the live goldfish in his earring? Who was he?

Jade Oh wow. He was weird. He showed me his scar.

She goes back to her pad. The others look at her

Maggie And?

Jade Oh, nothing. It was very big. He used to weigh two hundred and fifty pounds, but he had this operation and they cut miles and miles of intestines out of him and so now he's thin and handsome and really ready to cat around, you see, except that he suddenly has this strange compulsion to only sleep with very fat women, which he doesn't understand, but there it is, so that's why he wouldn't go to bed with me. (*She returns to her pad. A silence*)

Maggie Oh.

Gideon Well, did he have a name?

Jade (*looking up*) I guess.

Maggie We should crack this case in no time.

Irene returns down the stairs, carrying a blanket. She takes it into the study

Nadine (*as Cynthia*) Please, Nadine. (*As herself*) In a little while.
Irene I found this. It's colourful. (*She starts to drape it over Rick*)
Sammy Don't. (*He bends down, touches Rick's face, then turns away*)

Irene covers the body

Nadine sings the chorus of Bob Dylan's Blowing in the Wind

Nadine (*speaking*) Goodbye, Rick.

Nadine rises and walks into the living-room. Irene looks at Rick's body, then the doorway into the living-room. She points to the door

Irene It had to be this way.
Sammy What?
Irene The bullet. The gun. From this direction.
Sammy It could have come from the window.
Irene Not the way he was hit. The killer had to be standing in the doorway. Oh, here I go, always trying to solve everything. I should leave it to the police.

Irene and Sammy walk into the living-room

Maggie (*putting down her pad*) I'm sorry, I don't remember anyone else.
Gideon Yeah. This is it for me.

Clay takes their pads and then collects the pads from Roberta and Jade

Clay About nine names between us ...
Gideon He'll be miles away by now.
Roberta Unless he's right here in this room.

Maggie goes to Roberta and offers him a cup of egg-nog

Maggie Listen, have some egg-nog. It will help you relax.
Roberta They're gonna think it's me.
Maggie What do you mean?
Roberta Nothing. But I didn't do it.
Maggie Nobody here did it.
Roberta How do you know?

Clay (*to Jade*) I'd like to photograph the study. Would you like to help?
(*He picks up his camera*)

Jade I don't want to go into that room again. (*To Gideon*) Do you have
some dope?

Gideon Sure. (*He hands Jade a joint*)

Jade (*lighting it*) It's not right in that room. It's all past, you know what
I mean? Rick is no longer in the 'now'.

Maggie Guess that says it as well as anything.

Gideon offers her a joint

No thanks. The egg-nog's all whisky. Well, I suppose I'm a free lady
now. Are you interested?

Gideon Hey, his body's still warm.

Maggie So is mine. Ahh, I'm kidding. Don't let it get you.

Gideon Sit down.

Maggie I'm nervous. I want to pace. (*She sits*) There, are you upset? You
really liked him, huh?

Gideon I guess. Liked him, didn't like him at all, loved him, you know?
I just can't figure out what's going to happen *now*. Forget it. You're not
too upset.

Maggie Do you know how many guys have left me? A lot. Of course, I've
never had one get shot before.

*Clay walks to the door between the living-room and the study. Irene is
there, looking at the door. Jade walks up to Clay*

Jade I don't think we should go into that room anymore. Not unless we
put the body on a pyre and burn it ... They do that in India, and they seem
to know best. (*She wanders off again*)

Clay (*to Irene*) You're sure the bullet came from here?

Irene Fairly sure.

Clay Wonder why we didn't hear anything.

Irene There was so much noise in the garden.

Clay I guess. And then the killer walked calmly back into the party ...
Perhaps we should look for the gun.

Irene Why?

Clay Well, if it were a man, he'd have a problem. Everything's so skin-
tight these days. There's no place to hide a gun.

Irene So maybe it was a woman.

Clay I don't know. (*He takes her hand*) You're very pretty. You're the type I never get into my films.

Irene (*pulling her hand away*) Gosh. Is that an offer?

Suddenly, the Lights flicker and dim, then go out. It is dark, completely dark. Nothing can be seen

Sammy Now what?

Irene Oh dear, is it another earthquake?

Maggie Nothing's moving.

Roberta The killer's cut the power!

Clay This happens sometimes after a tremor. A delayed power-failure.

Irene What a city!

Jade It's very sexy like this. Who am I next to?

Roberta Hands off, creep.

Nadine (*as Cynthia*) Let's get out of here. Please.

Maggie Who was that? I didn't recognize that voice. There's a stranger in this room.

Nadine That was Cynthia.

Maggie Oh, her.

Gideon Hey, you're really jumpy.

Maggie Yeah. Well, why not? It's Goddamn dark in here, and there's a dead body in the next room ...

Gideon Calm down, calm down ...

Irene Aren't there any candles?

Jade Maybe we should all meditate.

Nadine There were lots of candles in the garden.

Clay Where's my camera?

Irene You just had it.

Clay But I put it down. I can't find it.

Gideon No-one's going to steal your camera.

Irene Why don't we get the candles from the garden?

Roberta Nobody leaves this room!

Nadine (*as Cynthia*) Now Roberta, if we all go to the garden we can each take a candle; that way, we will *all* be together and then we will *all* have a lot of light.

Maggie Was that Cynthia?

Nadine Yes.

Maggie Just checking. She sounded like an analyst, didn't she?

Jade If we meditate, we'll have an *inner* light.

Clay I know I put the camera somewhere. What's this?
Roberta Hands off, creep.
Clay Sorry.
Maggie (*an ungodly screech*) HOLD IT! DON'T MOVE!
Sammy What is it?
Gideon What happened?
Maggie My contact lens slipped out.
Sammy Jesus!
Jade What a bummer.
Maggie I have it! It's on my finger.
Irene You scared me half to death.
Maggie OK. Which way to the garden?
Gideon Come on. Take my hand. Here.
Sammy Whose hand is this?
Gideon I guess it's mine.
Sammy That's fine with me.
Maggie I have somebody's hand. Is it yours?
Nadine It's mine.
Maggie Cynthia?
Nadine Nadine.
Gideon We can just feel our way to the door ...
Jade This is fun.
Sammy I have the door. Come on ...
Roberta Nobody try any tricks ...
Sammy This way ...

Slowly, hand in hand, they all feel their way into the garden, except for Clay, who is still searching for his camera

Clay It's amazing ... I'm such a well-ordered person, and then I lose everything. I was sure the camera was right here. Irene? Are you still here? If I find the camera, maybe you'll really think about it, about doing a little film for me. Irene? She isn't here. Is *anybody* here? Maybe she'll do a little film for me ... What's this? A typewriter? I must be in the study. The camera's in the living-room. She's very attractive. I'd like to see her breasts. I'd like to film her in bed with someone. As long as I have my camera ... How could I lose it? You just don't lose something like that, it doesn't make any sense ...

A shot rings out. There is a long silence. Voices are heard in the garden

Maggie (*off, in the garden*) What was it?
Gideon (*off, in the garden*) Stay here.

Gideon enters, holding a burning candle. He moves the candle around the living-room. Maggie enters, followed by Irene and Sammy. They are also holding burning candles

Gideon Don't come in.
Sammy It's empty.
Maggie Well, it *sounded* like a shot.

Jade and Nadine enter, followed by Roberta. They also hold burning candles

Sammy (*pointing to the study*) Do you think?
Jade Don't go in there.

Gideon, Sammy, Maggie and Irene enter the study. Gideon moves his candle around, Roberta and Nadine join them. Jade stays in the living-room. Gideon's candle throws a light on Clay's body. Clay is lying on the floor, dead

Irene Oh dear Lord!
Nadine Is he dead?
Gideon (*bending over the body*) Yes.
Maggie So much for the guest list.
Irene I guess it's one of us.

CURTAIN

ACT II

A half-hour later. The house is ablaze with candles of all shapes and sizes, bathing the living-room and study in an eerie light. A fire burns in the fireplace

Clay's body has been covered with a blanket. It remains on the floor of the study, near Rick's body

Nadine is sitting at a table, playing Monopoly with Cynthia

Gideon, Jade and Maggie are on the floor. Gideon has a tray in front of him on which is some white powder, arranged in three sections. He takes a rolled-up dollar bill and sniffs one section of powder through it. Jade and Maggie are awaiting their turns

Irene sits in the study. She is staring at the two bodies and is deep in thought

Roberta is outside, in the garden, with his back against the garden door, either protecting or imprisoning the people inside

Sammy comes down the stairway, carrying a huge candelabra

Maggie Enough candles, already. The house is gonna burn down.
Sammy This is the last. I promise.

Sammy takes the candelabra into the study

Gideon Beautiful! (*He dreamily passes the cocaine and the dollar bill to Jade*)

Jade snorts cocaine during the following

Sammy (*in the study — to Irene*) Where shall I put this?

Irene What?

Sammy The candelabra.

Irene I don't know. Anywhere. Did you check the cars?

Sammy There's no way to get to them. A tree is down in front of the garage.

Irene Can't we walk?

Sammy Walk? Down the canyon road?

Irene Sure.

Sammy It can take us hours, and even then we might not find a cop. The phones are never out for long. Relax.

Irene It's all so confusing.

Sammy What is?

Irene (*pointing to Rick and Clay*) This.

Sammy Try not to think about it. (*He puts the candelabra on the desk*)

Irene We were *all* in the garden, weren't we?

Sammy (*lighting the candles*) Who knows? It was dark. I don't know where *you* were for sure. Do you know exactly where I was?

Irene I guess not. But aren't you worried?

Sammy You mean that one of us is bonkers? Listen, I've been around so many nuts, I figure my life is almost always in danger. Last week, this bum, very drunk, wobbled up to me in the street and said, "Hey, mister, if I had a gun, I'd kill you" and I looked at him, and realized, sure 'nuff, if he *had* had a gun, he'd have killed me. Once a week, honey, once a week, you come across someone like that. So there's a lunatic running amok in this house? What can you do?

Irene But there might be clues. Maybe we can figure out who it is.

Sammy Well — I figure who can figure? Of course, now that I'm Catholic I have some security. *We* get to go to Heaven. If I were still Jewish, maybe I'd worry.

Sammy goes into the living-room. Jade hands the tray to Maggie

Maggie You know, all the parties I've been to, and I've never done coke before. I always pass it by.

Gideon and Jade look at her

You don't want to give me any hints?

Gideon and Jade are, at the moment, too high to talk

If I don't like it, can I keep the dollar bill? (*She puts her hand against one nostril*) Here goes ... (*She sniffs some powder. A pause*) I like it better in cans.

Sammy sits down next to Maggie

Sammy Is there any left?

Maggie shakes her head

What a drag. I don't think they'll offer me any coke at the monastery, not for a while, not until they're sure I'm cool. How y'doing?

Maggie just stares at him

You're doin' all right.

She lights a joint

Roberta comes in from the garden and looks around

Roberta Now, nobody try a run for the door, you hear me?

The others ignore him. Nadine is moving her player-piece on the Monopoly board, and counting the steps as she moves

Nadine One, two, three, four ... shit. (*As Cynthia*) New Hampshire! That's mine. Four hundred dollars. (*As herself*) You're just lucky. (*She gives herself four hundred dollars*)

Roberta goes to Nadine and moves a chair beside her. He is drinking egg-nog. During the last part of the conversation Maggie wanders over

Roberta Hey, listen, lady, can we talk?
Nadine Sure.
Roberta I been watching you. I don't think you're the one.
Nadine (*smiling*) Oh, you can't be too sure.
Roberta Hey, don't get me wrong. I don't mean you're not crazy, you *plenty* crazy, but I don't think you're a killer. The others — it's written all over them, you gotta watch them like a hawk.

Nadine I will.

Roberta Listen, lady, can I ask you a favour?

Nadine Sure.

Roberta When the police come they'll arrest me.

Nadine (*as Cynthia*) Why do you say that?

Roberta Huh? Oh, it's that voice trick of yours. Yeah, well, see, I'm easy to pick on.

Nadine (*as Cynthia*) What makes you think that?

Roberta It's just the way it is.

Nadine (*as Cynthia, very much the analyst*) You must have reasons. Try to remember.

Roberta Well, you're working on the dock, unloading bananas, you know, and the guys, they throw things down your bra, and when a shipment's missing, they say it's you, that you need the money for a new pair of stockings; you're just a target, that's all.

Nadine (*as Cynthia*) How long have you had these feelings? (*As herself*) Cynthia, don't! (*To Roberta*) What's the favour?

Roberta Call this number for me. My wife. Let her know before the papers get to her. (*He hands Nadine a slip of paper*)

Nadine OK. (*As Cynthia*) You didn't say you had a wife.

Roberta Yeah. I do.

Nadine (*as Cynthia*) What are your feelings about her?

Roberta I love her, what d'you think? I mean, she's been very understanding, *very* understanding.

Nadine (*as Cynthia*) Do you still maintain relations with her?

Roberta What kind?

Nadine (*as Cynthia*) Sexual.

Roberta Hey, lady, what do you think I am, some kind of lesbo?

Maggie pulls a chair over and sits down. She is very stoned

Maggie You know, I tried to be a lesbian for a whole year. Really worked at it. But it didn't take. It's a shame because men have so many problems... (*To Roberta*) You're well out of it. Believe me. It's a fucking *smart* choice.

Roberta Don't talk dirty to me.

Sammy walks over to them

Maggie Oh. Sorry. My second husband liked me to talk dirty. He was like a little boy. I don't get it— what's so great about being a little boy again?

Sammy Well, honey, it wasn't much fun the first time around, so we're just trying to get it right. (*He pulls over a chair and sits down*)
Nadine (*as Cynthia, to Sammy*) Did you have a difficult childhood?
Sammy Of course. Didn't you?
Nadine (*as Cynthia*) We're not discussing my childhood.
Sammy We're not discussing *my* childhood either. What is this?
Nadine (*as Cynthia*) Why are you resisting me?
Sammy What are you going on about?
Maggie You know something, you *are* resisting her. What are you hiding?
Roberta Maybe you should tell!
Nadine Oh God, Cynthia, you have a *group* going!

Irene walks into the living-room from the study. She is very excited

Irene Something's on the tape!

The others look up, startled

Sammy What?
Irene Something's on the tapes he made! Something that gives it away. That's why he was killed.
Gideon Who was killed?
Irene Clay.

The others just stare at her

   There are two dead bodies in there. Doesn't anyone care?
Sammy What was on the tapes?
Irene I *don't* know. That's just it. But it's the logical reason for his being murdered. When he would show the tapes, he'd discover the identity of Rick's killer. So the killer had to get Clay first, don't you see?
Maggie I did an Agatha Christie play once, and I didn't understand a word of it.
Irene I'm *very* serious.
Sammy Oh, honey, it just doesn't pay.
Nadine (*as Cynthia*) Why do you have a *need* to be serious?
Irene You're *all* crazy.
Roberta Watch it, lady!

Irene Shouldn't we try to look at the tapes?
Gideon (*getting up, still dreamy*) Oh, man, it's over anyway. It's all over.
What's the use? (*He pulls Jade up*) Come here ...

*Gideon takes Jade to the fireplace, holding her hand. They sit in front of
the fire. Irene walks to the garden door and stands looking into the garden*

Can you understand what I'm trying to tell you? It's no more. Man, they
were the best days of my life. You know what it was like up until then?
How could you know? When were you born? Ahh, you missed it, you
were born too late. You missed all those boring years when nothing
happened and everyone looked the same. Do you know how ugly I was?
Oh yeah, it's true. I mean, it's not true, I wasn't ugly at all, but people
thought I was, because I looked strange, exotic, freaky, you know, not
like anyone else. Kids used to laugh at me in the streets and they were
right, my clothes never fit. You try to be skinny back then, they didn't
make clothes for you, no-one was skinny. But suddenly over night, the
world changed, and *all* the clothes were being made for you, and strange
was fine, and freaky became a compliment, and I was beautiful, and the
same kids in the street pointed to me and waved and said, oh wow; and
my mind, too, my *mind* suddenly made sense; off-centre was centre, or
there was no centre or *something*, but it all fit in. I fit in. And being with
Rick's band, sure, that made sense, I was an *asset*—oh yeah, those were
good days ... but it's all speeding up, speeding up and slowing down at
the same time, and I don't think I understand it anymore and if Rick's
dead, the times are dead, and what's going to happen to me? Do you
think I'll become ugly again? Am I going to have to change? I like it the
way I am! Oh, man, you're so spaced out ... do you know what I'm
saying?

Jade stares at him for a moment in silence

Jade This girl I know. She's twenty-two. She said when she was my age she
was making plaster casts of guys' cocks. She said it was better then — in
the old days ...
Gideon Yeah. Like that kind of thing doesn't happen anymore. I mean,
that's six years old. A lifetime.
Jade Want me to do it?
Gideon What?

Jade Make a plaster cast of your cock. Then maybe you'll know it's all right, what was then can still live in the 'now'. Oh yes. Let me do it. Rick has some plaster in his game room. I'll mix it, then you come upstairs and I'll go down on you and get you real hard and we'll put you in the cast, and you won't be unhappy anymore. Oh yes. Let me do it. Please.
Gideon Do you think you can?
Jade (*standing up*) I'm getting the plaster. I'll call you when it's ready.

Jade goes upstairs

Irene (*turning around, once again excited*) Also — Clay was a lawyer! You forget that! He handled all of Rick's legal work. That included Rick's will, and heaven knows what else, and so he knew better than anyone who had the most to gain from Rick's death, and who had the most reason to shut him up. (*The others look at her*) Oh, for Pete's sake, don't you *care*?

Disgusted, she turns back and stares at the garden

Nadine (*as Cynthia*) I believe Sammy was telling us about his childhood.
Sammy I most certainly was not.
Nadine (*as Cynthia*) Is your hostility based on the fact that I'm a woman?
Sammy I'm not hostile.
Nadine He really *isn't*, Cynthia. Can't we go back to Monopoly? (*As Cynthia*) Why are you defending him? Why are you angry at me?
Sammy She's not angry at you.
Nadine (*as Cynthia*) Why are *you* defending *her*? Is this a conspiracy? (*As herself*) There's no conspiracy. (*As Cynthia*) This man is trying to comfort me.
Roberta I ain't a man no more.
Nadine (*as Cynthia*) Well, I can't help that. You should have come to me sooner.
Roberta What's she talking about?
Sammy Don't pay any mind.
Nadine (*as Cynthia, to Sammy*) You hate me. You hate your mother. You hate Marilyn Monroe.
Sammy I *loved* Marilyn Monroe.
Nadine (*as Cynthia*) Because she was a *parody* of woman, that's why! She wasn't real!

Maggie What was wrong with Marilyn Monroe?

Nadine (*as Cynthia, crying*) I tried to help, all my life I tried to help ... but suddenly no-one would listen. (*As herself*) It's all right. Cynthia, it's all right. Don't get upset. Please.

A loud alarm bell rings in the study

Irene What's that? (*She runs into the study*)

Roberta Burglar alarm?

Irene (*walking out of the study holding an alarm clock*) It's only a clock. (*She turns the alarm off*) Actually, it's Rick's clock. Why do you think he set it for two twenty-three?

Sammy (*joking*) Maybe it's a clue.

Irene Well, anything could be a clue.

Sammy You mean there's a message there in the time? Two twenty-three?

Gideon But only *that* clock says two twenty-three. How about the others?

Sammy What others?

Gideon There's a clock in every room upstairs.

Maggie (*standing up*) Then there are lots of clues.

Irene You're making fun of me.

Maggie Let's get them. We can compare all the clocks, see what time they're set for, and find out whodunnit. Come on.

Irene This is really serious.

Maggie Come on. We'll take a room apiece.

Maggie goes upstairs, Sammy and Gideon follow her

Roberta Hey — don't try any funny stuff!

Roberta goes upstairs after the others

Irene I'm very serious.

She turns, opens the garden door, and moves into the garden

There is a silence

Nadine (*as Cynthia*) Nadine? (*As herself*) What? (*As Cynthia*) I'm sorry.

(*Silence. As herself*) I told you. (*As Cynthia*) I know. (*As herself*) That's all over. (*As Cynthia*) I know. (*Silence. As herself*) You're safe here. Safe with me. I'm always going to take care of you. No-one's ever going to hurt you again. I won't let them. You're never going to leave me. Are you? Please, don't leave me. It's awful ... alone. Cynthia? (*As Cynthia*) What? (*As herself*) Please ... (*As Cynthia*) I won't leave. I promise. (*Silence. As herself*) This house isn't good anymore. (*As Cynthia*) Ghosts. (*As herself*) What? (*As Cynthia*) It has ghosts. They want to talk to me. (*As herself*) Should we go? (*As Cynthia*) Yes. Now. (*As herself*) Cynthia, did ... (*As Cynthia*) What? (*As herself*) Nothing. (*As Cynthia*) Say it. (*As herself*) No. (*As Cynthia*) We have no secrets. (*As herself*) Don't we? (*As Cynthia*) What do you mean? (*As herself*) You hated Rick. (*As Cynthia*) That was hardly a secret. (*As herself*) Then did you ... did you kill him? (*Silence*) Oh, Cynthia, was it you? I'm praying, praying that it wasn't. Tell me the truth. Did you kill Rick? (*As Cynthia*) No. I didn't. (*As herself*) Then who did? You know, don't you? (*As Cynthia*) No. (*As herself*) Tell me ... (*As Cynthia*) It's only a possibility. (*As herself*) A possibility? (*As Cynthia*) A thought. (*As herself*) Well, what is it? (*As Cynthia*) You won't believe me. (*As herself*) I will. (*As Cynthia*) No. You won't. (*As herself*) I'll try. Please Cynthia. It's important. *Tell* me. Who killed Rick? (*As Cynthia*) All right. I think it's ——

A shot rings out. Nadine falls over the Monopoly board, dead. Silence. Nadine (as Cynthia) sits up. Another shot rings out. Nadine (and Cynthia) fall over the board again, this time definitely dead

    Irene runs in from the garden

    Maggie, Sammy, Gideon and Roberta come down the stairs. They each hold an alarm clock. They all stare at Nadine. Suddenly, the Lights come on again, full blast. It is very bright. They look at each other

Silence

    Jade comes to the top of the stairs. She appears to be unaware of what's happening

Jade The plaster's ready.

Gideon continues to look at Nadine. He appears to be so stoned that he can't take it all in

Gideon!

Gideon backs away from Nadine's body, and walks backward, up the stairs, his hand reaching out for Jade. She takes his hand, and they go off

Maggie walks to the sofa. She sits. She looks at her clock

Maggie Mine says four-thirty. (*She drops the clock on the sofa*)

Sammy kneels by Nadine's body

Sammy I should have told her about my childhood. What did I have to lose? It would have made her happy. I should have dredged up some old memories for her. (*He sings, softly*)
> Oh today we'll merry merry be
> Oh today we'll merry merry be
> Oh today we'll merry merry be
> And have some homintashin.

We used to sing that at Purim. When I was a child, Purim was my favourite holiday. I should have told her that. She wanted to help.

Maggie I remember that song. I was thirteen and I dressed up as Queen Esther and won second prize in the Hebrew School costume parade. That was the start of my career. (*She sings, with spirit*)
> Oh today we'll merry merry be
> Oh today we'll merry merry be...

Maggie⎫ (*together*) ⎧ Oh, today we'll merry merry be
Sammy⎭   ⎩ And have some homintashin.

Irene What's homintashin? Oh, for heaven's sake, listen to me! I don't care about *that*. (*She points to Nadine*) I care about this.

Sammy (*softly*) So do I. (*He looks up*) Are there more blankets upstairs?

Sammy walks up the stairs to the second floor

Roberta (*looking at Nadine*) She was all right. (*To the others*) I warned her about you guys.

Irene Well maybe now we can all start to seriously worry.

Maggie I don't feel too well.

Irene She knew. Of course! She had to know who the killer was. That's why she was shot. I mean, she understood human behaviour; she was an analyst. That is, she thought she was an analyst. Gosh, it gets confusing. (*She looks around*) And she was shot from there — from that window. (*She points to the window next to the stairs*) That would seem to be the right angle. Don't you think?

Silence

Maggie Who knows?

Irene Well just look.

Maggie I don't want to look.

Irene And there's a veranda right below the window.

Maggie (*turning around*) But we were all upstairs.

Roberta (*to Irene*) Yeah, except you were in the garden. (*To Maggie*) You make a note of that. She was in the garden, right next to the veranda.

Irene You can reach the veranda just as easily from any of the upstairs windows. It could have been any one of us, including you.

Roberta You watch your step, lady. You're not going to pin this on me.

Irene I'm just pointing out that any one of us could have been the killer.

Maggie The rate things are going, I hope it's me.

Roberta Yeah? Maybe it is.

Maggie Now what's *that* mean?

Roberta Just letting you know that I have my eyes open.

Maggie Wonderful.

Irene (*looking up at the restored lights*) Do you think the phone's back?

Maggie (*getting up and going to the phone*) Let me try. I need some activity. (*She holds the receiver up*) Nothing.

Irene Well, it's silly to just stay here. I can go and get help. Maybe I can get a ride down the road.

Maggie Sure, walk out the front door and never be seen again! We don't play it that way, darling. We can *all* go to the police.

Irene Good. *That* makes sense. Let's do it. Where's Sammy?

Sammy comes down the stairs, holding a blanket

Sammy Right here.

Maggie And Gideon?

Sammy Upstairs. Getting a blow job.

Maggie Well this is no time for *that*.

Sammy Fine. Tell it to him.

Irene But it's a matter of life and death.

Sammy Honey, sometimes getting a blow job is a matter of life and death.

Irene But *this* is serious.

Sammy You keep saying that. *Nothing* is serious. (*He puts a blanket over Nadine's body*) Nothing.

Maggie How long is Gideon going to be?

Sammy (*looking up*) I'm supposed to answer *that*?

Irene We've got to go to the police.

Roberta Not me, lady. I ain't walking in no police station. They'll never let me out.

Maggie We're certainly not going to leave you here alone!

Sammy (*to Irene*) So — see? — you're back where you started. So why even start? Relax, honey, everything works out for the best.

Jade comes to the top of the stairs. She is trembling and crying

Jade Help!

Irene Oh no.

Jade Help. Please ... somebody come and help ...

Maggie Gideon!

Jade I didn't mean for it to happen ...

Maggie Is he ... ?

Jade Yes. Stuck.

Maggie *What*?

Jade He's stuck in the plaster.

Sammy starts to laugh

I can't get it off. I can't get it out. He's stuck. I don't know what to do.

Sammy (*still laughing*) I'll take a look.

Sammy runs upstairs

Jade comes down into the living-room. Irene turns to Maggie

Irene Everything has a pattern. If we can find a pattern, maybe we can figure out who did it.

Jade I did it. I sucked his cock and put the plaster over it and it got stuck.

Irene Darn it, that's *not* what I mean!

Sammy comes down the stairs

Sammy He's stuck all right.

Jade How do we get it off?

Sammy Beats me. It's *not* unattractive.

Irene (*to Maggie*) And then there's the gun. Do you think that one of us
is really wearing a gun at this very minute? I doubt it. There *has* to be
a hiding place. The sensible thing to do would be to search the entire
house, top to bottom ...

*Gideon appears at the top of the staircase, naked, except for a plaster
cast clinging to his erect penis*

Gideon Oh man, this is grim. (*He comes down the stairs*)

Irene Good heavens!

Jade My girlfriend never mentioned anything like this happening, but
she's been into mescaline pretty heavy and only remembers things in
flashes ...

Gideon (*going to Maggie for comfort*) Maggie.

Maggie *Now* you come to me. It's too late.

Gideon Rick had *his* done six years ago and nothing went wrong. What
will I do?

Sammy Won't it get loose if you get soft?

Gideon Maybe. But the plaster is stimulating.

Roberta I can take care of it. Just wait a minute.

Roberta rushes up the stairs

Maggie (*very bemused*) Can't we just *pull* it off?

Gideon glares at her

No, huh?

Gideon (*to Jade*) I tried telling you — it's all over. The good times are
gone.

Maggie (*holding up a pen*) Would you like me to autograph it?

Jade I don't think you should blame me.

Gideon Well — look at it.

Jade I just wanted to make you happy. I mean, I can do that, *in my way*.
(*She stares at Gideon*) I'm glad I'm not old.

Roberta comes down the stairs, holding an axe

Roberta OK. This will do it. (*He holds up the axe*)
Sammy Jesus!
Roberta (*going to Gideon*) I'll crack it open.
Gideon (*backing away from him*) Sure you will!
Roberta Listen, punk. I'm trying to help.
Gideon Stay away from me.
Roberta It won't hurt any.
Gideon Just keep your distance.
Roberta (*going toward him*) I'll have it off in no time flat.
Gideon He's *crazy*! (*He runs into the garden*)
Maggie Roberta, put that thing down!
Roberta I know what I'm doing.

He goes into the garden

Maggie I'll bet he does.
Sammy Roberta!

Maggie and Sammy go after Roberta, into the garden

Irene I don't understand it. Three people are lying dead and you're all playing games.
Jade Oh, it's fun to play games.

Gideon runs in from the garden

Gideon Somebody's got to stop him.
Jade I think we're supposed to call him 'her'.

Roberta runs in, wielding his axe

Gideon Stay away!

Gideon runs upstairs

Roberta Hey, come back. This is for your own good ...

He runs upstairs after Gideon. Maggie and Sammy run in from the garden

Sammy Roberta, since when have you gotten helpful?

He runs upstairs after Roberta

Maggie (*to Irene and Jade*) Some night, huh?

Maggie follows Sammy upstairs

Irene Look, I'm getting out of here. I'm going to find a police station and bring back some help. You can tell the others for me. (*She gets her handbag from a chair*)
Sammy (*off, upstairs*) Roberta, where are you?
Maggie (*off, upstairs*) Gideon?

Irene walks out into the garden

Jade Oh, look at all the clocks. (*She picks up a clock*) My father used to collect alarm clocks. I don't know why people collect things. It's silly to have possessions. You never know where you're going to be from one moment to the next.

A shot rings out. Jade falls to the ground, the alarm clock in her hand. The alarm goes off. Jade is dead. A pause

Gideon, wearing a towel, bounds down the steps

Gideon Jade! It came off! I saw Roberta running around the hallway swinging his axe, and it just *shrivelled*. Isn't it wonderful what fear can do? Jade? (*He looks around for Jade*)

Irene comes in from the garden

Irene I heard a shot.

They both see Jade's body. Gideon bends down and turns off the alarm

Sammy comes down the steps

Sammy What happened?
Gideon It came off, and Jade's dead.

Maggie comes down the steps, behind Sammy

Maggie I don't want to look. My stomach hurts.
Gideon She was just a kid. Beneath the feathers. It's all shit, man.
Maggie And I have *such* a headache.
Irene I'll bet the bullet came from that window again.
Maggie *So shut the window* !
Irene There's no need to shout.
Maggie People are dropping like flies. I *want* to shout.

Sammy sits in a lotus position near Jade's body and begins to chant

Sammy (*chanting*) Ommm …
Gideon Somebody here is on a really bad trip.
Maggie It's not me. OK, I admit I once was very jealous of young girls.
   But then I had my eyes lifted … (*She moves to stand in front of the
   garden door*)
Sammy Ommm …
Irene (*looking at the others*) Somebody here … (*She stops herself, then
   turns to the garden door*) I was on my way to … (*She starts to move
   toward the door, but sees Maggie is standing in front of it, and suddenly
   thinks better of it*) I better get another blanket.

She walks upstairs

Maggie She thinks it was one of us.
Gideon Yeah. (*He starts up the stairs*)
Maggie Where are you going?
Gideon I'm still filled with plaster.
Sammy Ommm…
Gideon I have to wash.
Maggie I wish people would stay in one spot.
Gideon You do?
Maggie Don't look at me that way! *You're* the one with the motive.
   You're the one who got stuck.

Gideon goes upstairs

Sammy Ommm…
Maggie Is that all you can say?

Sammy Ommm...

Maggie I know what that is. That's Hindu. You're a total religious nut, aren't you? It doesn't matter *what* religion.

Sammy Ommm...

Maggie And religion, like sex, is the prime cause of murder.

Sammy Ommm...

Maggie So it could easily be you.

Sammy Ommm...

Roberta (*off, upstairs*) Hey, fellow, where the hell are you?

Maggie It's not safe upstairs ... It's not safe downstairs. It not safe. (*She sits on the steps*)

Sammy (*in a trance*) It's safe here, in my heart. It took a long time, but it's at rest. You know what we're going to do, years from now, our monastery? We're going to open our gates and walk into the world, and the world will pretty well have smashed itself up by then, and we're going to pick up the pieces. When it's all over, we'll come out and pick up the pieces. I see it, here in my heart, clearly. We'll walk about the land, setting things right again, and there will be mountains and sunsets and rivers. There will be rivers, and hopes and plans and thoughts, and the days that follow will be rich with creativity and joy and wonder ... (*Silence—then he holds his head*) Sorry. (*He looks up*) Was I someplace else?

Maggie More or less.

Sammy rises and walks to the other side of the room

Maggie Where you going?

Sammy Putting out the candles.

Maggie Don't leave me.

Sammy I'm just over here.

Sammy starts to blow out the candles. Maggie follows him around

Maggie I figured it out. The pattern. They were *alone* when they were killed. Except for the killer. You can't leave me.

Sammy Honey, at this point, don't even trust *me*.

Maggie I don't. I just don't want to be alone. I've never trusted anyone. I didn't trust my husbands, I didn't trust Rick ... I just didn't want to be alone. I *need* people even though I don't like them.

Sammy You can trust in God.

Maggie Yeah. Where'd that get *you?*

Sammy This far.

Maggie Not interested. God is too conventional. Those old things don't work anymore.

Sammy So what does?

Maggie Pizzazz. (*A pause*) A lot of smoke clouds. Glitter. All the wrong things. They work.

Sammy heads for the study door

Where you going?

Sammy To the john.

Maggie You can't.

Sammy I *can't?*

Maggie You can't leave me alone. You promised.

Sammy I didn't promise. (*He walks into the study*)

Maggie (*following him*) I'll go with you.

Sammy I'll just be half a minute. Relax.

Maggie *How?*

Sammy opens the bathroom door. Maggie starts to follow him in

Sammy What are you doing?

Maggie You're not going to leave me alone.

Sammy Look, all I want is a nice, quiet piss.

Maggie Well go ahead.

Sammy By myself. Some things you do by yourself. Just stand by the door. Right there. I'm only a few feet away.

Maggie You're sure?

Sammy Yes. Think of something calm and soothing. OK? (*He brushes his hand across her forehead*) Try —just for a minute — to be at peace.

Sammy exits into the bathroom and closes the door

Silence

Maggie I can't think of a single thing that's calm or soothing. Nothing! What do you mean, *peace?*

A shot rings out. Maggie grabs her stomach. Her body wavers, falters then steadies

Oh my God! It missed! (*She feels her body*) I *think* it missed. Of course
it missed. You don't get shot and not feel something. A little sting
maybe, but *something.* Hey — how about that? It fucking well missed!
Sammy? Did you hear that? (*She opens the bathroom door*)

Sammy falls out. He is dead

Sammy! But it's not possible. Not in there. (*She looks in the bathroom*)
A window! (*She kneels, cradles Sammy's body in her arms.*) Well,
listen, kid, you're probably in the best place, you know? (*She sings
softly, rocking him back and forth*)

> Oh today, we'll merry merry be
> Oh today, we'll merry merry be
> Oh today, we'll merry merry be …

*She stops. She stares at the study door. She rises and goes to the door, looks
out and can see the garden door. There is a clear avenue of escape. She
tiptoes out the door to the living-room, then starts to walk to the garden
door, at an increasingly rapid pace. Finally she is running. Suddenly she
stops cold in mid-step*

Damn it. (*She falls to her knees*) Goddamn it! (*She searches the floor*)
Why? Why can't they make a contact lens that will stay in? Come on,
where the hell are you? This is no time to fall out. Jesus! Where are you?
I'm not running into the police station wearing glasses. No way. Oh!
Come on! Bastard! I've got to get out of here. I've got to look good for
the morning papers. Come on! (*Her hand touches something*) *Gotcha!*
(*She stands up in triumph, holding a tiny lens on her finger*) I'm in
business!

*A shot rings out. Maggie stands for a moment in disbelief. Then she falls
to the floor, dead*

Silence

The telephone rings

> *Roberta appears at the top of the stairs, still holding the axe. He looks
> down into the living-room. The telephone continues to ring. Roberta
> walks down into the living-room, swings the axe and brings it crashing
> down upon the telephone wire. He severs the wire*

Silence

Roberta throws the axe down on top of the dead phone. He goes to a chair and takes a purse from it. He goes to a mirror, looks into it, and adjusts his make-up. He takes a little pillbox hat from the closet and puts it on. He takes another look, makes sure he's proper, and then walks to the garden door. He opens the door

A shot rings out. Roberta falls into the garden, dead

Silence

Irene comes down the stairs, trembling and carrying a blanket. She enters the living-room, stands a moment, then goes to the study. She looks at Sammy's body. She returns to the living-room, and looks at Maggie's body. She turns to the garden and looks at Roberta's body. She drops the blanket to the floor

Gideon appears at the top of the stairs. He glances at the bodies beneath him

Irene and Gideon stare at each other

Gideon Why?
Irene You tell me.

Gideon walks down the stairs. Irene backs away

Gideon It's all over.
Irene Is it?
Gideon Yes. I don't mind now.
Irene Mind what?
Gideon What's going to happen
Irene What *is* going to happen?
Gideon You know. (*Pause*) I'm waiting.
Irene Is there some way I can appeal to you?
Gideon What about?
Irene I have two children.
Gideon It doesn't mean anything.

Irene begins to back away toward the garden door. Gideon follows

Irene They have no-one to take care of them. Their father's in Asia. He'll be there for six months.
Gideon What does it matter?
Irene It matters! They need me.
Gideon Why talk ?
Irene I didn't know that my husband would be away so much. But then I never planned to marry into the military. War — killing — is repellent to me. I went on peace marches. Does that surprise you? Before I met Barry …
Gideon There's nothing left to say.
Irene But then I fell in love. Please, I beg you …
Gideon I've made up my mind.
Irene I have two children …
Gideon And nothing can change it.
Irene And a husband I love…
Gideon It's all over.
Irene (*shouting*) *No* !

She runs from the room, into the garden

Gideon Don't run away. I've made up my mind. It's over. *You have to kill me* !

A shot rings out

(*Smiling*) Oh wow! (*He falls to the floor, dead*)

Silence

Irene walks back into the room. She looks at Gideon's body

Irene It doesn't make sense. (*She bends down and touches Gideon's body, then pulls at it*) Gideon! Is this some kind of joke? (*She rises*) I didn't do this. I didn't kill him. I didn't kill *any* of them. (*She looks at the other bodies*) Everything *has* to make sense. You know that. Think it through. (*She sits on the steps*) I didn't do it. I know I didn't do it. (*Silence*) Right now, at this moment, I don't remember doing any of this. That's the clue.

I don't remember. Oh, for heaven's sake, this is silly. I didn't do it. (*Pause*) It's not silly. There is logic in everything. And there is always an answer. Just think it through. I've read case histories. A person's mind can be separated into sections. One can block out the other. I've read about that, so it has to be true. Maybe there are two parts of me. Oh, that's nonsense. No, it's not. It's *possible*. And this part doesn't remember the other one, the one that kills. But I didn't do it. I *had* to do it. There's no-one else. They're all dead. Gosh, if I could only remember... if I could only remember holding a gun or pulling a trigger or *something*. The gun. There has to be a gun. Where did I put the gun? I don't *have* a gun. It couldn't have been me ... (*Pause*) I had reasons. Lots of reasons. Rick! He's always been the same. So wild and free. And sensual. My goodness! He attracted me. Now, that's upsetting, isn't it? It has to be. So — there's a part of me that could kill him. Well it did. Obviously, it did. *But it didn't.* And Clay was making very improper advances. He wanted to put me in a dirty film. Sure. That other part of me could do it. It had a reason. Nadine — well, there was *really* a split personality; she'd catch on to me in no time. So that other part of me killed Nadine. And Jade ... that little girl flaunted her promiscuity. That other part of me didn't like that. See, there's a pattern. And Sammy, because he kept making fun of me, *this* me, whenever I wanted to go to the police. And Maggie, because she was so *loud.* That's reason enough. And Roberta— Roberta was just there, by that time, when did it matter? And Gideon because he was the *only one left.* It was easy. The veranda outside looks into all the rooms and I didn't have to be too cautious, everyone was so stoned and out of it ... It was so easy. All those flower-pots on the veranda! Of course. What a perfect place to hide the gun. It all fits! It's all clear. It all has logic. It *was* me. I did it! I killed Rick, I killed Clay, I killed Nadine, I killed Jade, I killed Sammy, I killed Maggie, I killed Roberta, I killed Gideon ... (*She rises, crying*) Oh thank God! Thank God! *It makes sense!* It was me!

A shot rings out

Irene Shit.

Irene falls to the ground, dead

Silence

CURTAIN

FURNITURE AND PROPERTY LIST

ACT I

SCENE 1

On stage: STUDY
Sticks of white, orange and green make-up
Purple sash
Silver bracelet
Gold bracelet
Necklace of turquoise and coral
Knife

LIVING-ROOM
Chairs
Sofa
Table. *On it*: cups
Coffee table. *On it*: writing pads, pens
Telephone

Personal: **Rick:** blood sacs

SCENE 2

Off stage: Video camera and lights (**Clay**)

Personal: **Gideon:** joint, lighter
Maggie: glass of egg-nog
Roberta: cigar

SCENE 3

Off stage: Large bowl of egg-nog (**Maggie**)
Burning candle (**Gideon**)

Burning candle (**Maggie**)
Burning candle (**Irene**)
Burning candle (**Sammy**)
Burning candle (**Jade**)
Burning candle (**Nadine**)

ACT II

Set: Burning candles of all shapes and sizes

STUDY
Blanket over **Clay's** body

LIVING-ROOM
On table: Monopoly set (open, in mid-game)
Tray. *On it*: white powder arranged in three sections
On a chair: purse
In closet: pillbox hat

Off stage: Huge candelabra (**Sammy**)
Alarm clock (**Maggie**)
Alarm clock (**Sammy**)
Alarm clock (**Gideon**)
Blanket (**Sammy**)
Axe (**Roberta**)
Blanket (**Irene**)

Personal: **Gideon**: rolled-up dollar bill, plaster cast, towel
Sammy: box of matches
Roberta: slip of paper
Maggie: pen, contact lens

LIGHTING PLOT

Practical fittings required: video camera lights

Interior and exterior. A study and living-room with garden backdrop. The same throughout

ACT I, SCENE 1

To open: Spot on **Rick** in study

Cue 1	**Rick** falls to the ground, dead *Black-out*	(Page 1)

ACT I, SCENE 2

To open: Full general lighting

Cue 2	A rumbling sound *Flicker lights, snap off, snap on*	(Page 4)
Cue 3	**Jade**: "Rick's dead." *Black-out*	(Page 5)

ACT I, SCENE 3

To open: Black-out

No cues

ACT I, SCENE 4

To open: Full general lighting

Cue 5	**Irene**: "Gosh. Is that an offer?" *Flicker lights, then black-out*	(Page 15)

ACT II

To open: General eerie effect; fire burns in fireplace

| *Cue* 6 | Everyone stares at **Nadine** | (Page 26) |
| | *Snap on full lighting* | |

EFFECTS PLOT

ACT I

Cue 1   **Rick's** face is bathed in ecstasy   (Page 1)
           Gunshot

Cue 2   Lights rise on **Rick's** house   (Page 1)
           Party sounds from garden

Cue 3   **Nadine:** "I care."   (Page 4)
           Rumbling sound

Cue 4   Lights flicker, go off, come on again   (Page 4)
           Rumbling sound gets louder, as if the house is shaking

Cue 5   **Clay:** " ... it doesn't make any sense ... "   (Page 17)
           Gunshot

ACT II

Cue 6   **Nadine:** "All right. I think it's —— "   (Page 26)
           Gunshot

Cue 7   **Nadine** (as Cynthia) sits up   (Page 26)
           Gunshot

Cue 8   **Jade:** " ... from one moment to the next."   (Page 32)
           Gunshot

Cue 9   **Maggie:** "What do you mean, *peace*?"   (Page 36)
           Gunshot

Cue 10   **Maggie:** "I'm in business!"   (Page 36)
           Gunshot

Cue 11   **Maggie** falls to the floor, dead. Silence   (Page 36)
           Telephone rings

Cue 12	**Roberta** chops the telephone wire *Telephone stops ringing*	(6)
Cue 13	**Roberta** opens the garden door *Gunshot*	(Pa
Cue 14	**Gideon:** "You have to kill me!" *Gunshot*	(Page
Cue 15	**Irene:** "*It makes sense*! It was me!" *Gunshot*	(Page 3

PRINTED IN GREAT BRITAIN BY
THE LONGDUNN PRESS LTD., BRISTOL.